GET OUT ALIVE!

ESCAPE FROM KILLER CLAWS

Julie K. Lundgren

Published in the United States of America by Cherry Lake Publishing Group
Ann Arbor, Michigan
www.cherrylakepublishing.com

Reading Adviser: Beth Walker Gambro, MS, Ed., Reading Consultant, Yorkville, IL

Photo Credits:
© Robert Cinega/Shutterstock, cover, (tiger), © Vishal shinde/Shutterstock, cover, (deer), © klyaksun/Shutterstock (graphic on cover and throughout book); © Cassette Bleue/Shutterstock, speech bubbles throughout; © Nazarkru/Shutterstock, yellow bursts throughout; © JFS07/Shutterstock, page 3; © Volodymyr Burdiak/Shutterstock, page 4, and page 6 (bottom); © neelsky/Shutterstock, page 5 (top), ©miroslav chytil/Shutterstock, page 5 (bottom); © ivector/Shutterstock, page 6 illustration; © Evgeniyqw/Shutterstock, (top), © Omer Farooq Bin Mehfooz/Shutterstock, page 7; © Julian W/Shutterstock, page 8; © alicja neumiler/Shutterstock, (top), © Sourabh Bharti/Shutterstock, page 9; © shivaram subramaniam/Shutterstock, (top), © Atiwich Kaewchum/Shutterstock, (bull) page 10; © Suntisook.D/Shutterstock, (top), © Anuradha Marwah/Shutterstock, page 11; © 555Prakash/Shutterstock, page 12; © sanjayda/Shutterstock, (top), © Sourabh Bharti/Shutterstock, page 13, page 18 (bottom), and page 21 (deer); © CHAKKYZ/Shutterstock, page 14-15; © Arpan9620/Shutterstock, (top), page 15; © Danita Delimont/Shutterstock, page 16; © Vaitheeswaran 78/Shutterstock, page 17, and page 19 (bottom); © Karl Weller/Shutterstock, (top) page 18; © abdullahyaseen295/Shutterstock, (top) page 19; © Amitabh d/Shutterstock, page 20; © pmvtisl/Shutterstock (top;© Dr. Meet Poddar/Shutterstock, page 22 (top), © Fernandodiass/Shutterstock (POW!); © Harshvardhan Sekhsaria/Shutterstock, (top), © DW34/Shutterstock, page 23.

Produced for Cherry Lake Publishing by bluedooreducation.com

Copyright © 2026 by Cherry Lake Publishing Group

All rights reserved. No part of this book may be reproduced or utilized in any form or by any means without written permission from the publisher.

Library of Congress Cataloging-in-Publication Data has been filed and is available at catalog.loc.gov.

Printed in the United States of America

Note from Publisher: Websites change regularly, and their future contents are outside of our control. Supervise children when conducting any recommended online searches for extended learning opportunities.

About the Author

Julie K. Lundgren grew up in northern Minnesota near Lake Superior. She delighted in picking berries, finding cool rocks, and trekking in the woods. She still does! Julie's interest in nature science led her to a degree in biology. She adores her family, her sweet cat, and Adventure Days.

Contents

NIGHT BEAST 4
I AM A SUPER PREDATOR! 8
I AM SUPER PREY? 12
GET OUT ALIVE! 16
FIND OUT MORE 24
GLOSSARY 24
INDEX 24

NIGHT BEAST

In the night, alone and silent, a predator hunts its prey. It's a Bengal tiger!

WE KNOW TIGERS BY THEIR ORANGE AND BLACK STRIPES.

A Bengal tiger roams forests and swamps. It often hunts in places thick with grasses and plants.

SIBERIAN TIGERS ROAM COLD, WILD AREAS IN RUSSIA AND CHINA. THEY ARE SLIGHTLY BIGGER THAN BENGAL TIGERS.

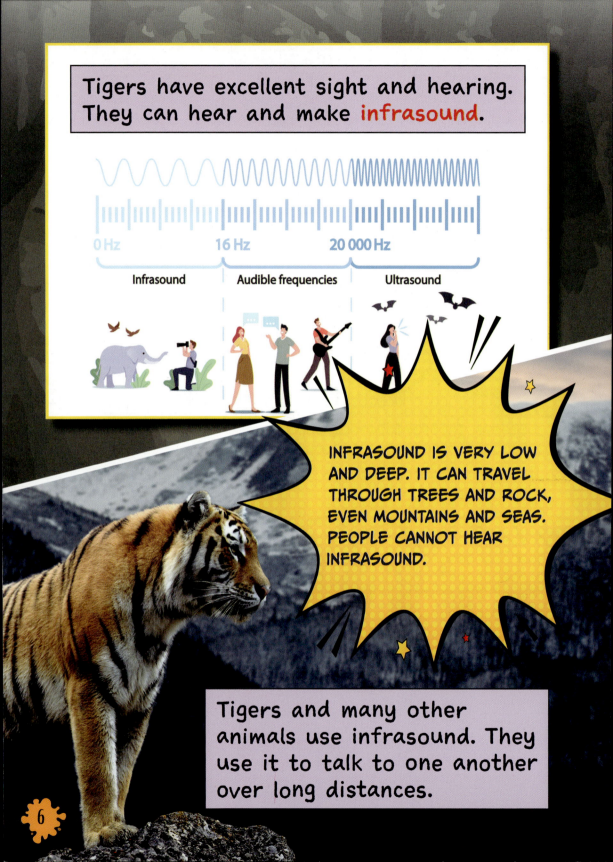

Like other cats, tigers see well in dim light.

RARE WHITE TIGERS ARE A TYPE OF BENGAL TIGER. BENGAL TIGERS HAVE YELLOW EYES. MOST WHITE TIGERS HAVE ICY BLUE EYES.

MY SHARP TEETH GRAB PREY AND SLICE MEAT FROM BONES.

MY STRONG JAWS GRIP LARGE PREY BY THE NECK. MY MUSCLES DRAG HEAVY ANIMALS EASILY.

TIGERS HAVE KILLER CLAWS, ONE AT THE END OF EACH TOE. THEY HAVE A **DEWCLAW** ON THE INSIDE OF EACH FRONT LEG. DEWCLAWS HELP THEM CLIMB AND GRIP PREY.

Tigers kill to feed themselves and their young.

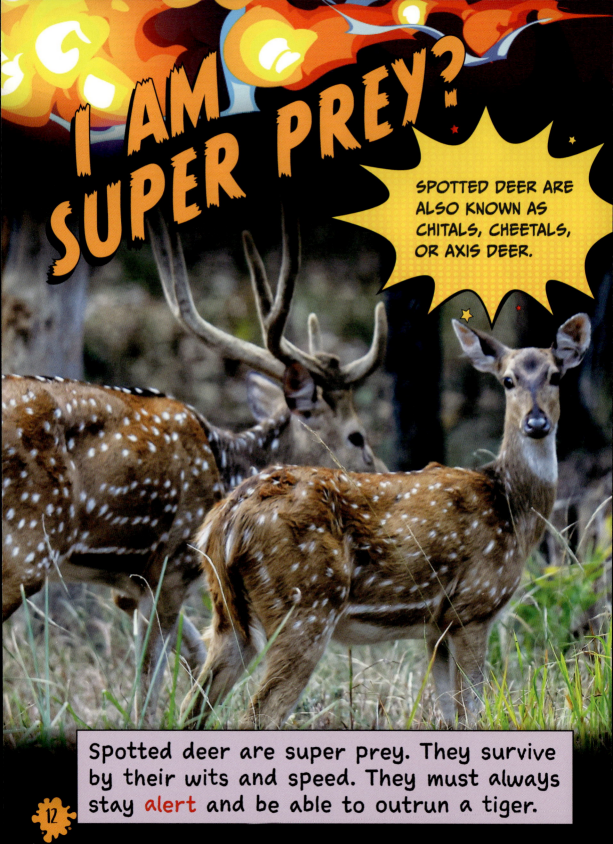

I AM SUPER PREY?

SPOTTED DEER ARE ALSO KNOWN AS CHITALS, CHEETALS, OR AXIS DEER.

Spotted deer are super prey. They survive by their wits and speed. They must always stay alert and be able to outrun a tiger.

ANTLER

Male deer use their antlers to stab attackers. All deer sometimes smash predators with their hooves.

HOOF

FEMALE DEER DO NOT HAVE ANTLERS.

GET OUT ALIVE!

TIGERS AMBUSH THEIR PREY.

A young Bengal tiger crouches low and still when it spots a deer herd.

The deer stay close together. They nibble plants. So far, the day has been quiet.

The tiger moves toward the prey. It stays hidden.

HUMANS CAN SEE A TIGER'S ORANGE STRIPES. SPOTTED DEER CANNOT. THEY SEE SHADOWS AND LINES THAT LOOK LIKE GRASSES.

The tiger creeps closer. If the deer notice the tiger before it is in **kill range**, they can easily run away.

The deer don't see the tiger yet!

Freeze! The deer now know something is near. They stand very still.

The tiger pauses for a few seconds to recover.

In those seconds, the deer puts on a burst of speed. It rejoins the herd. Safe!

Find Out More

Books

Dickmann, Nancy. *Bengal Tigers*, Tucson, AZ: Brown Bear Books, 2019

Kline, Carol. *All about Asian bengal tigers*, Hallandale, FL: Mitchell Lane, 2020

Websites

Search these online sources with an adult:

Tigers | National Geographic Kids

Spotted deer | Britannica

Glossary

alert (UH-lert) quick to notice danger

ambush (AM-bush) to hunt by sneak attack

detect (dih-TEKT) find and identify, often using the body's senses

dewclaw (DOO-klaw) on tigers, the claw on the fifth toe of each front paw

infrasound (IN-frah-sownd) sound below the lower limit of our hearing, made by some animals and machines

kill range (KILL RAYNJ) the area immediately around prey within which the predator has a good chance of success

pounces (POWN-sez) suddenly leaps or springs onto prey

predator (PRED-uh-ter) an animal that hunts and eats other animals

prey (PRAY) animals that are hunted and eaten by other animals

swamps (SWOMPS) forested wetlands that can have deep standing water

swipe (SWAHYP) hit with a swinging blow

Index

ambush 16, 21
antlers 13
dewclaw(s) 11
herd(s) 14, 16, 23

infrasound 6
legs 10, 22
plants 5, 17
prey 4, 9, 11, 12, 16, 18

run 8, 19, 21
speed 8, 12
stripes 4, 18